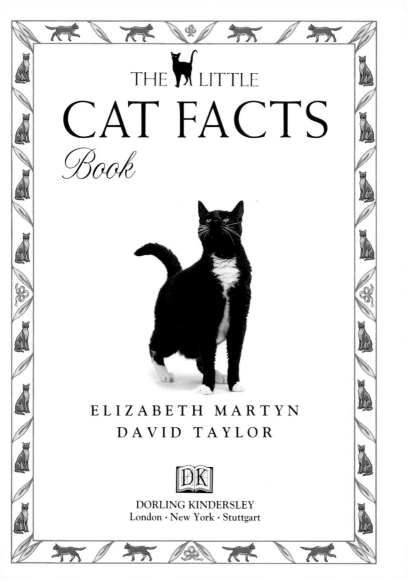

THE LITTLE
CAT FACTS
Book

ELIZABETH MARTYN
DAVID TAYLOR

DORLING KINDERSLEY
London · New York · Stuttgart

A DORLING KINDERSLEY BOOK

PROJECT EDITOR Candida Ross-Macdonald

DESIGNER Camilla Fox

MANAGING EDITOR Krystyna Mayer

MANAGING ART EDITOR Derek Coombes

PRODUCTION Lauren Britton

First American Edition 1993
10 9 8 7 6 5 4 3 2 1

Published in Great Britain by Dorling Kindersley Limited.
Distributed by Houghton Mifflin Company, Boston.

ISBN 1-56458-263-9
Library of Congress Catalog Card Number 92-56495

Reproduced by Colourscan, Singapore
Printed and bound in Hong Kong by Imago

CONTENTS

CREATIVE
Cats

How the sinuous feline figure has padded into art, novels, poetry, and films down the ages.

CATS IN EARLY ART

The beauty of the feline form has been an inspiration to artists since brush was first put to papyrus.

Ancient civilizations knew the cat, and featured it in both domestic and religious art. Over 3,000 years ago, cats with the lean bodies and sharp faces still typical of Oriental felines are included in Egyptian wall-paintings and manuscripts. Scenes on the walls of tombs unearthed in the Valley of the Kings show cats with tabby coats at play, hunting, and living with families as domestic pets.

CHURCH CATS

The domestic cat is generally not to be found in European paintings of the Middle Ages, but it does appear in some medieval bestiaries. These were collected descriptions of real and mythical creatures, often beautifully illustrated, and always with the high moral tone of medieval Christianity. Domestic cats also put in an appearance in much church architecture, and cats of wood and stone can be found beaming down from capitals, curled snugly under misericords, and adorning the pews and choir stalls. These carved cats may owe their existence to fables or pagan stories known to masons and carpenters, rather than to any Christian doctrine.

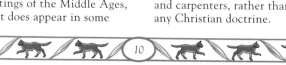

Left: Medieval bestiary cat
Above: Detail from Bassano's
"Last Supper"

SINFUL SYMBOL

With the Renaissance, cats begin to creep into paintings. Scenes of the Holy Family feature cats, as do many depictions of the Annunciation and the Nativity by artists like Tintoretto, Rubens, and Titian. Sometimes the cat is simply an innocent witness, but it can be a sinister symbol of the devil.

Leonardo da Vinci sketch detail

CATS ON CANVAS

All styles of art continue to include the cat, and some artists have had an almost exclusively feline output.

Around the turn of the century, French painters sometimes included a cat with their portrait subjects. Edouard Manet's "Olympia" shows a small black cat at the feet of the naked figure reclining on the bed. The great Impressionist Auguste Renoir added cats to several of his female portaits, emphasizing the sensuous nature of his work.

STREET LIFE
Theophile Steinlein is famous for his bold, colorful posters and paintings, many of which include striking cats painted from his observations of the rooftop and alley cats of the Montparnasse area of Paris.

Gwen John, a British painter who lived in France in the first half of this century, came to enjoy the company of felines more than that of people, and her paintings of cats are now collectors' items. Some of them feature serene cats posed with pensive young women, while others are captivating studies of her own cat.

EASTERN ART
Regarded as sacred and lucky in Japan, the cat has naturally played an important role in Japanese art. Feline lightness is a perfect subject for the delicate precision of Japanese style, and there are many elegant and

Left: Renoir girl with a cat
Right: Ishikawa cat on a mat
Below: Cat napping, by Sei

witty studies of cats snoozing on cushions, playing with their mistresses (often geishas), or loitering with intent by the goldfish pool. Many of the best were by the 18th-century artist Ichiyusai Kuniyoshi, whose studio was overrun with cats. They would even make themselves comfortable in the folds of his kimono as he painted. More modern Oriental artists have followed in the tradition of his paintings, if not the living arrangements.

FABLED FELINES

From fables and folklore to modern day children's stories, character cats have appeared in print.

Cats have always captured the imagination. Whether it's because of their air of mystery, their aloof attitude, or their firm belief in their own charm, cats have insinuated themselves into stories as wily tricksters, detached observers, and symbols of luck or of sinister forces.

FABLE AND FAIRYTALE
Although Aesop is renowned for his fables, next to nothing is known about the man himself.

A Greek who is thought to have lived in the 6th century B.C., he may have been a slave with a penchant for wild adventures. In his fables, cats hold their own against foxes, mice, birds, and monkeys. One of the legendary cats known in Western fairytales is Puss in Boots, created by Charles Perrault in the 17th century, but based on an older tradition of magician cats, or *matagots*, in French folklore.

Left: Lear's Owl and Pussycat go to sea
Right: Fable cat and company
Below: Alice and kittens by Tenniel

CHILDREN'S CLASSICS

Children first meet cats in rhymes like "The Owl and the Pussycat" and stories like Beatrix Potter's *Tom Kitten*. The Cheshire Cat is a fascinating feline from *Alice's Adventures in Wonderland*, while two kittens become the White and Red Queens in *Through the Looking-Glass*. Books offer dozens of cats for young readers to discover.

LITERARY CATS

As a favorite pet of the literati, the cat has been portrayed often and vividly in poetry and prose.

Many a writer has pored over the page to the accompaniment of soft purring from a feline companion. Something in the quiet presence of a cat seems to soothe the troubled artist and help the creative spirit.

POETIC PAWS

In the poems of *Old Possum's Book of Practical Cats*, T.S. Eliot points out that cats are rather like people: "Some are better, some are worse, but all may be described in verse." This volume of poems is now famed as a stage musical. An 8th-century Irish poet praised his predatory cat Pangur Ban – "Hunting mice is his delight, Hunting words I sit all night" –

and poets from Swinburne to Stevie Smith have lauded the cat ever since. Many of them, including Christina Rossetti and the 19th-century rural novelist Thomas Hardy, penned lofty valedictory odes dedicated to the memory of departed pets. One of the more famous cats in modern poetry is Mehitabel, of the *Archy and Mehitabel* poems by Don Marquis. The perfect poetic representation of the devil-may-care cat, she dismisses any troubles with a nonchalant "wotthehell." She also asserts, with unshakable confidence in her own lineage, that in an earlier life she was Cleopatra.

Left: *Poe's Black Cat*
Above: *Feline fan Johnson*
Right: *Hemingway at home*

COMPANIONS OF HONOR

Edgar Allan Poe was fond of felines, although the cats that he featured in his work are – like the stories themselves – distinctly creepy. The smug cat is summed up in Saki's classic short story *Tobermory*. When a well-meaning professor teaches him to speak, the cat of the title abandons discretion and reveals all the secrets of a group of friends gathered for a weekend party, causing chaos and dismay, and then departs with a self-satisfied smirk.

Samuel Johnson's cat, Hodge, is familiar to any student of his life, but it is less well-known that the great lexicographer's amanuensis and biographer, Boswell, was allergic to the pampered pet, and "suffered a good deal" on account of him. Never renowned as a man of moderation, Ernest Hemingway didn't stop at just one feline acolyte: at one time he had 25 cats at his home in Cuba, and created his own breed. The cats still have the run of his house, which is now a museum.

SCREEN STARS

Whether cast as the star or in a nominally supporting role, cats always know how to steal the show.

Cats are seldom cast as the starring role in films, although they often take center stage in cartoons. Yet they hypnotize the camera when they stroll on screen, and have even upstaged some of Hollywood's great legends.

CREEPY CATS
Understandably, perhaps, cats are often cast in horror and mystery films. In the classic Ingmar Bergman film *Don Juan*, the devil takes on the form of a black cat in order to spy on the hero's seductions, and Batman's adversary, Catwoman, has always been accompanied by a suitably slinky feline, on both television and the silver screen.

In two of the Bond films a fluffy white Chinchilla accompanies the villain Blofeld – a case of beauty and the beast. In a slightly more sympathetic line are avenger cats. A pet whose owner is killed does away with the greedy relatives scrabbling for the estate in *Shadow of the Cat*, and cats turn the tables on a murderer in *The Eye of the Cat*.

PET PRIZES
Every feline starlet dreams of a PATSY award to decorate the basket. The Picture Animal Top Star of the Year trophies are the animal world's equivalent of the Oscars, and no fewer than nine cats have

Left: A kitten tastes La Dolce Vita
Right: A cat has nine lives, but You Only Live Twice
Below: Cathouse cat from Walk on the Wild Side

walked off with the prestigious prize since it was first given. Among the most memorable of these top-notch performers was the simply named Cat, who co-starred with Audrey Hepburn in *Breakfast at Tiffany's*.

Originally, the award covered only film stars, but the entrance qualifications were later widened to include television performers. This allowed Morris, America's favorite feline due to his role in cat food commercials, to become an award winner. Like many other actors before him, Morris went on to run for the post of President, but unfortunately with less success.

Cats

ON RECORD

*Cats of all shapes and
sizes, from the original
wild cats to the common
and uncommon breeds
we see today.*

FIRST DOMESTICATED CATS

Cats have been loved and nurtured as hearthside companions for over 5,000 years.

The first true cats, hunters that walked on their toes, evolved around 12 million years ago. Continental drift had isolated Australia before this, so the continent has no native members of the true cat family. South America was in a similar situation, until big cats spread from North America.

SMALL SCALE

Only in Europe and Africa did the smaller wild cats that were the ancestors of the domestic cat evolve. The Ancient Egyptians adopted the African wild cat as a pet and sacred animal. The remains of mummified cats unearthed in many ritual burial sites are identifiable as the African Wild Cat, as are depictions in wall paintings and scrolls. So resilient are the cat's genetic patterns that some modern breeds, such as the Abyssinian, still bear a striking resemblance to their ancestors.

TRAVELING CATS

The habit of keeping cats spread from North Africa throughout the Middle East with traders, although it may have developed separately some time later in China. Cats reached Italy by 900 B.C., and crossed Europe with the Romans, arriving in Britain about A.D. 100. They reached America in the 17th century, taken on the ships of settlers.

Left: The Abyssinian, a cat with old-fashioned looks
Right: Ra as a cat slays the serpent of darkness in a scroll from Ancient Egypt
Below: Tabby cat from an Italian abbey

CHANGING FASHIONS

The earliest domestic cats were shorthaired and tabby, like their wild cat forebears. The different colors and patterns of the coat first occurred as mutations and were preserved by people breeding from them. Longhaired cats developed in the rugged mountain lands of southern Russia, Afghanistan, and Iran, possibly from crossbreeding with the longhaired European wild cat, and spread to Turkey. They arrived in Italy in the 16th century and from there spread through Europe like their shorthaired cousins.

MINICATS AND MONSTER CATS

Most breeds of the domestic cat fall within a fairly narrow size range: large enough to fill a human lap comfortably, but still small enough to squeeze through an enticing hole in the fence. On either side of this range, however, there are a few unusual breeds. There would be room for two tiny Singapuras on most people's laps, since these diminutive felines can weigh as little as 4 lb (1.8 kg), the females being especially small. On the other hand, watch out if a Maine Coon decides to take a snooze on your knee: the males of this gentle-giant American breed commonly weigh in at a hefty 14 lb (6 kg).

SLEEK AND SLENDER
The svelte and dainty Tonkinese is a Siamese-Burmese cross, and it combines the charms of both in miniature form.

POCKET PUSS
Sweet natured and sociable, with a smooth, satiny coat, the Singapura originated – as its name suggests – in Singapore. Most litters contain only three kittens, which are slow to mature, and the breed is rare outside Asia.

Hardiest Cat

Built to withstand the toughest conditions, the Norwegian Forest Cat has a warm, woolly undercoat and a waterproof top coat that repels the heaviest downpour. With the males commonly weighing 15–20 lb (7–9 kg), this cat likes the space of the outdoor life. Although its name suggests wild origins, the breed has in fact been happily domesticated for centuries, and while it needs freedom, it also enjoys human company.

Gentle Giant

American farm cats crossbred with Persians brought over from Europe produced the Maine Coon.

VENERABLE CATS

Cats are considered to be adolescents at just six months of age, and adults by the time they are one year old. This breakneck rate of development slows down throughout the feline lifespan, so a cat of nine or ten years of age can be regarded as middle-aged, and cats that reach their twentieth birthday are, in human terms, centenarians. Many domestic cats have been known to survive into their mid-twenties and beyond in good health, and the cats holding the male and female world records for feline longevity were Methusalahs indeed, both living well into their thirties.

Past It
At 15 years, this Siamese tom could still sire young. Queens generally stop producing kittens by 12 years of age, although some females have given birth in their twenties.

Fading Away
Some cats tend to become obese with age, but many grow thin. Cats like this Oriental Ticked Tabby, although looking wasted, live on in good health for years.

Senior Citizens

The life expectancy of the domestic cat used to be set at around 12 to 15 years, but improvements in both diet and veterinary care have gradually increased this. Nowadays, a lifespan of 16 to 20 years is nothing unusual. Accidents are frequently to blame for untimely deaths, so if at all possible keep your cat safely away from dangers such as traffic.

Old Lady

Non-pedigree cats generally live longer than pedigree cats, and females like this contented puss outlive males by up to two years on average. Neutered or spayed cats tend to outlive their intact counterparts, perhaps because they lead more sedate lives, without the hurly-burly of duels and parenthood to wear them out.

RARE CATS

Although the common cat has enough appeal for most of us, some will always seek the rare and precious. Breeders can never resist creating new feline variants, partly for the challenge and partly for the undoubted financial reward. In its 1986 Christmas catalog, the Nieman Marcus in Beverly Hills offered California Spangled cats for sale at $1,400 apiece. Another top-drawer cat is the Tiffany, bred from Persians crossed with Burmese, and every bit as exclusive as its name. Other cats are simply difficult to breed: Tabby Persians, for example, are much more scarce than their shorthaired counterparts.

CALIFORNIA CAT
The California Spangled is a new breed derived from Nile cats and Malayan house cats, with just a sprinkling of Angora, Abyssinian, and Siamese thrown in.

HALF-WILD CAT

An Asian Leopard Cat-domestic tabby cross, the Bengal has the beauty of a wild animal with the affability of a family pet.

FLOPPY FELINE

The Ragdoll is named for its habit of becoming totally limp when picked up. It does not, as is sometimes claimed, have an unusually high pain threshhold.

COUNTRY AND COLOR

Just as prophets are never recognized in their own lands, so the common cats of one place may be prized elsewhere. Egyptian Maus are house cats in their native land, where *mau* simply means cat, but highly valued in America. Very rare in Europe, they may be confused with Oriental Spotted Cats, which were once called Maus. Conversely, black or white varieties of Russian Blue are bred almost exclusively in New Zealand. The numbers of some cats are naturally limited. Tortoiseshell and blue-cream breeds are usually female only. Very few male kittens are born with either of these coat patterns, and virtually none of them survive into adulthood.

CURIOUS CATS

There are hundreds of myths and legends about cats, but feline folklore attaches itself especially to those whose appearance is out of the ordinary. The squint of the original Siamese cats, for example, was attributed to their habit of staring at the treasure that they guarded in Oriental temples. The Manx is said to have arrived at the Ark so late that Noah accidentally closed the door on its tail, hence its bereft hindquarters. Nobody knows how the cats came to the Isle of Man, but the tailless gene has become predominant and the cat still flourishes there.

CURLY COAT
The extraordinary wavy fur of the Devon Rex is soft and very short, but the breed is reasonably hardy and doesn't seem to feel the cold.

Good Luck

The Japanese Bobtail has a short, curled, pom-pom tail. The breed occurs naturally throughout Japan, China, and Korea, but is rare outside the Far East. In Japan, cats with tails that divided at the end were thought to harbor evil spirits, a belief that may have encouraged the breeding of short-tailed cats. When seated, the Bobtail often raises a paw in a "beckoning" gesture, associated with good luck (see page 54).

Missing Tail

Manx cats with no tail at all are called Rumpies. Those that have a residual tail, like this one, are known as Stumpies, Stubbies, or Longies, depending on the length of the tail. The gene that causes this tailless state is also responsible for more serious defects. As a result, if two Rumpies mate their offspring are very unlikely to survive.

Lop Ears

The Scottish Fold appeared as a mutation in a litter of farm cats in the 1960s. The ears present no problems to their feline owners, and these hardy cats make friendly pets.

PAMPERED
Cats

*Rich cats, bon vivants,
and the famous people
who have loved – and
hated – the cat.*

MILLIONAIRE MUTTS

Ever since humans first tamed cats the animals have been spoiled. The cats sacred to the Egyptian goddess Bast lived in splendor in her temples. In Japan, the Emperor Ichijo was so delighted with his own kitten he declared the cat to be a protected animal. The kitten was served by its own maid, and had all the privileges of a high-ranking court lady.

HOME COMFORTS

The rich still indulge their pets today. In the United States, stores sell cat-sized water beds, and salons offer cats massages or shampoo-and-sets. There are even marriage services on offer for true romantics. Who knows what cats, who nap anywhere and take fastidious care of their own coats, make of all this. Perhaps the feline psychiatrists now available have the answer.

Other investments in cats' comforts are just as outrageous. You can have a house built for your cat in any style you choose, or buy jeweled collars and heated beds. You can even buy a "cataerobic center," a home with platforms, toys, and scratching posts, that will stretch to the ceiling of a room for maximum climbing space.

Left: For pampered cats, a cataerobic center
Right: One of the top-of-the-range options for the truly houseproud cat

Where There's a Will

Some cats are born with silver spoons in their mouths, others inherit them. Cat owners have always shown great concern for their pets' lifelong security. Two 18th-century English aristocrats, the Earl of Chesterfield and the Second Duke of Montagu, both left their cats generous pensions. A century later, a French harpist left her two homes and an annuity to her cat, to show how much she had appreciated his critical comments on her playing. Unfortunately for the cat, the family challenged the will and won.

In this century, Charlie Chan – a former stray – was left a house and contents estimated to be worth $250,000. An American oil heiress used her fortune to help a whole community of cats: she left a bequest setting up a home for New York strays, where 125 cats could live in the lap of luxury. In 1988 in England, the wealthy Mrs. Walker left $5 million to an animal charity on condition that her cat be looked after until he died. She was soon outdone by Ben Rea, who left $12 million to three charities and the last of his many pet cats.

FAT CATS

There are big cats, enormous cats, and cats that are, quite simply, huge. Here are some of the fattest felines on record.

A self-portrait by the 18th-century Scottish artist John Kay shows his cat perching, with some difficulty, on the back of his chair. A gigantic creature, whose body completely covers the chairback, it was thought to be the largest cat living in all Scotland. Since then, there have been plenty of felines eager to push the fat cat record further up the scales. In the 19th century, the most well-off cat owners tended to spoil and overfeed their pets as much as they did themselves. Lithographs of the time show some spectacular specimens, including one oversized cat who lived in Oxford Street, London. It was recorded that, surprisingly, he was "rarely inconvenienced by his great bulk."

Cats in the 20th century have continued to waddle their way up the scales. Tiddles was a stray taken in as a kitten at Paddington Station in London. Tiddles spent his life draped across first one chair, and then two, as his weight climbed to 30 lb (13.6 kg). A refrigerator was installed at the station to store Tiddles' supply of his favorite foods: steak, rabbit, chicken, and kidneys all featured in his rather large diet. But Himmy, an Australian cat, leaves previous portly cats in his considerable shadow. Tipping the scales at a massive 46 lb (20.8 kg), Himmy found walking such a problem that his owner took to ferrying the fat feline around in a wheelbarrow.

WEIGHT PROBLEMS

The world's favorite cartoon cat is "I'm not overweight, I'm undertall" Garfield. The reality for fat cats is not as cheerful. Truly vast cats usually have a genetic or hormonal problem, and many die young. Most cats regulate their own weight well, but some lose their shape, and their liveliness with it. This is often the result of overfeeding and a lack of exercise. An indulgent owner may be to blame, but canny cats also beg at second homes. Fat cats have a shorter life expectancy than normal cats and, just like us, may have to calorie-count.

Left: Portly Victorian cat
Above: Garfield in Macy's Christmas Parade, New York
Below: The cat that got the cream

Cat Friends and Foes

Cats can inspire extreme reactions. Here are some of the people who have loved and loathed them.

Powerful people often keep cats, perhaps because they are always discreet. Sir Winston Churchill often attended to paperwork from his bed in the mornings, with Nelson, a black cat who was his closest companion through the worst war years, curled up on his feet. Churchill's last cat, Jock, was provided for in his great owner's will, and lived out his last days at Churchill's country retreat, Chartwell. There has been a cat by the name of Jock in residence ever since. Abraham Lincoln felt so sorry for three bedraggled cats spotted during a visit to the Civil War camps that he took them back to Washington with him. Slippers, President Roosevelt's cat, regularly attended glittering White House dinners. General Eisenhower, on the other hand, ordered that any cats seen on the grounds of Gettysburg should be shot.

THE RELIGIOUS LIFE

Many men of the cloth have made their cats their confidants. Pope Pius IX used to dine with his cat, and Leo XII adopted a kitten that was born in the Vatican. He named it Micetto and would cradle it tenderly against his immaculate white robes. Cardinal Wolsey, Henry VIII's Chancellor, was devoted to his cat, which would sit by him as he carried out his diplomatic duties. Another great cat-loving Cardinal was Louis XIV's minister, Richelieu.

*Left: Cat-fearing
Julius Caesar
Above: Napoleon
in heroic pose
Right: Cardinal
Richelieu and
companions*

FELINE FEAR

Ailurophobia, or fear of cats, leads some people to bizarre actions when confronted by a friendly feline. Napoleon Bonaparte, fearless in battle, was once found by his aides stabbing wildly at a tiny kitten that had roamed into his rooms. Julius Caesar and General Kitchener were other military leaders with this malaise. The composer Brahms took his antipathy further, and let fly with bow and arrow at any cat that passed his window.

Cat
ANTICS

*A compendium of
traveling cats,
acrobats, hunters,
military mascots, and
bringers of good luck.*

VOYAGING CATS

Intrepid cats hitch rides and use their uncanny
navigational abilities to find their way home.

It can be hard to believe some of the astonishing tales of cats finding their way home. Cats do have a kind of innate compass. We don't know how it works: it may be that cats are super-sensitive to Earth's magnetic field, or that they use the angle of the sun. But there is plenty of evidence that it does work.

In tests, cats have been taken blindfolded to unknown locations, then set free. They found their way home easily. This amazed the scientists, but would come as no surprise to some cat owners. Sugar, a Californian cat, hit the road when her owners moved three states to Oklahoma. Over a year after they arrived, they heard a familiar meow at the door. Sugar was back. Other cats show more attachment to a place than their owners. Tiring of the Parisian winter, Gringo decamped for his family's sunny holiday home in the south, where neighbors recognized the tourist from summer visits.

*H*OME AT LAST
As a kitten, Gribouille was taken from central France to southwest Germany. A patriotic cat, he absconded three weeks later. A trek of 21 months left him half-starved, with sore feet and infected eyes, but it brought him back home, where he wanted to be.

Left: Felix, traveling First Class rather than storage
Below: Tibs the station cat going home

HITCHING A RIDE

Some cats travel the easy way. Tibs, a station cat from Preston in northern England; got on the London train one day, to arrive wide-eyed in the big city. The adventuress was sent home on the next train. One cat sailed from Britain to Australia in a container with a Mercedes.

Jet-set Felix stowed away in an airplane hold in Germany, and flew to London, New York, Rome, Los Angeles, Rio, India, and Saudi Arabia. In just four weeks, she clocked up air miles equivalent to circling the world seven times. Cats survive these tough conditions by licking condensation for water and by keeping calm to save energy.

LEAPS AND BOUNDS

Cats are perfect hunting machines, moving silently, running swiftly, and performing breathtaking leaps with ease. Their spines have more vertebrae than ours, and are extraordinarily flexible. On average, a domestic cat can spring to five times its own height and still land safely.

The Long Drop

The feline ability to land safely has saved many a cat from an untimely end. Cats have plunged 200 ft (60 m) and lived. Many New York apartment dwellers keep cats, and pets inevitably take dives from time to time. Amazingly, of cats known to have fallen from skyscrapers, 90 percent survived. Cats used to be thrown annually from a tower in Ypres, Belgium, to show that they were not worshipped, and often they ran off unhurt.

Taking Off

The joints and muscles in the cat's powerful hindlegs are designed to give the maximum forward thrust in a leap. Clever cats stretch their legs and bodies out as far as possible – even down a wall – before they finally launch themselves into the air. This effectively reduces the distance that they have to cover in the jump itself.

Rightside Up

A cat dropped upside down from a mere 12 in (30 cm) can turn itself over in under two seconds and land on all four paws. First it rotates its forequarters and brings its head up, then it flips its hindquarters around and spreads its limbs, ready for landing. The horizontal spread of the body and the splayed legs also help to slow the descent.

Safe Landings

Whenever it is possible, a cat will spring forward in a jump, rather than go vertically downward. This allows it enough time to bring its hindpaws up so that they meet the ground with the forepaws, spreading the impact of the landing.

COURAGEOUS CATS

Famed, and sometimes unjustly despised, for their innate caution, cats can show remarkable fortitude.

It never pays to ignore your cat when it might be trying to tell you something. Cats make good smoke detectors with their finely tuned sense of smell, but they have also served as early warning systems for other dangers. Cats sense changes in air pressure and small vibrations in the land long before humans notice anything, a sensitivity that we sometimes think of as a sixth sense. In a village in the foothills of Vesuvius, a cat called Toto went to great lengths to wake his owners one night. Refusing to be appeased, Toto clearly wanted the family to follow him away from their home. They took the cat's forebodings seriously and left the house – which was engulfed in hot lava when the volcano erupted only hours later.

PRISON VISITORS
Faithful felines stand by their owners in times of trouble. Sir Henry Wyatt was governor of the Tower of London until he

Left: All in a day's work, and he wasn't paid danger money
Right: The Earl of Southampton and Trixie after their sojourn in the Tower at her Majesty's displeasure

fell from Henry VIII's favor and was cast into his own cells. He was close to starvation until his cat appeared at the window with a pigeon for supper. Henry VIII's daughter, Elizabeth I, in her turn incarcerated the Earl of Southampton in the Tower. But just when he was feeling utterly deserted, who should scramble down the chimney but Trixie, his cat. She stayed with her master until his release two years later.

CATS AND DOGS – AND MORE

Minstrel spent his life running the gauntlet of a line of police dogs. The dogs had to ignore distractions such as an arrogant feline strolling past.

Cats will also help other creatures. Mother cats have fostered baby squirrels and rabbits, abandoned puppies, and orphaned skunks. Fostering works best when the strangers are introduced soon after the mother's own kittens are born.

SUPERCATS

Unlike dogs, most cats turn up their noses at the idea of performing tricks, but some enjoy showing off.

Some cats show a natural aptitude for the unusual – for example, Turkish Vans are famed for their un-feline love of water. Most people who want a performing pet, however, must devote many hours to repetitive training. One American cat owner spent five or six hours of every day on teaching her pet to eat with chopsticks. It paid off: after an appearance on television, the cat was swamped with offers of work.

CAREER CATS
Arthur found fame advertising cat food, eating it with his paw. When he retired, a replacement was sought. Arthur II studied the technique for months, and the food has even been renamed in honor of its patron.

CLOWNING AROUND
In the 19th century, the cats of Signor Capelli's Circus braved high wire and trapeze, juggled, and took orders in three languages. George Techow's Performing Cats leaped through flaming hoops, pussy-footed along tightropes, and walked on their front paws. Techow took three years to bring a cat to its peak, and worked with two- to three-year-old cats, claiming that they had longer attention spans than kittens. More recently, the Moscow State Circus made a tour of Europe, bringing a troupe of cats that hurtled over obstacles, did "handstands," and played chess. Their trainer, Yuri Kouklachev, restricted

Left: Arthur's technique
Above: Yuri and his protegés
Right: Turkish Van in its element

training sessions to evenings, finding the cats to be more receptive to learning after dark.

Good trainers confirm that any attempt at training must be on the cat's terms. A game that a cat enjoys may be turned into a trick, but if the cat does not show an interest, it is best to forget the whole thing.

MIGHTY MOUSERS

Cats are by nature hunters. The playful pouncing that they enjoy is practice for those all-important hunting skills. While town cats have limited hunting opportunities, country cats dispatch prey ranging from mice and birds to water rats, frogs, and toads. Despite this carnage, cats seldom affect wildlife populations, although they can do untold damage on small islands, where it is hard for wildlife to reproduce. Hunting cats have always been able to find employment. Towser, a tabby working in a Scotch distillery's grain stores, killed over 25,000 mice in her distinguished 23-year career. Minnie, a cat with a taste for rats, polished off an average 2,000 a year over a six-year spell as resident ratter at a London sports stadium.

DEADLY GAME
Why do cats "play" with their victims? It may be to prolong the hunt or use up energy, or, with larger prey, to line up an accurate coup de grace.

Take Away

A cat that intends to eat its prey will usually carry it away to a safe place before starting its meal, or will make frequent checks for competition as it eats its catch.

Resourceful Ratter

In La Fontaine's fable The Cat and the Old Rat, the wily feline pretends to be tied up in order to catch the rats unawares. As Gustave Doré's engraving shows, only one old rat is shrewd enough to see through the ruse.

BEWARE OF THE CAT!

Cats once warded off both corporeal and spiritual enemies. In Egypt and the Far East, feline statues stood guard over tombs. In China, candles were lit in hollow statues, so that the eyes glowed eerily. The original Birman cats are said to have saved their temple from an advancing army. Today, cats are still kept in the temples of the Far East.

*O*LD PROFESSION
A young Buddhist acolyte cradles one of his temple's cats, a living example of an ancient tradition.

*F*EROCIOUS FLUFF
Even a normally placid Persian can be raised to anger. With ears flattened out of harm's way and teeth bared, there is no mistaking this feline's feelings.

Paws Off!

Cats usually avoid taking on a mismatched opponent. They use a variety of rituals, such as staring routines, vocal threats, and feinted attacks, to avoid fighting. Arching the back and raising the fur to increase apparent size, as this kitten is doing, are classic cat tactics. If left with no escape, however, even the smallest cats have a formidable armory at their disposal.

Combative Cats

Catfights are usually short and vicious, a mass of fur as the combatants use their forelegs to grapple and their powerful hindlegs to kick, as well as attacking with their teeth. Usually there is one dominant cat in any neighborhood, but in a few cases these get out of hand and terrorize the area. Their targets may not only be other cats: although not as common as the postman-devouring dog, cats that attack people are not unknown. Bruno, a British mixed breed, bullied local dogs and defeated even animal rescue societies.

LUCKY CATS

The cat has been a symbol of luck, both good and bad, throughout the world. It's easy to see why people have believed the cat to have mystical powers. Its amazing night vision, its silent movement, and its acute senses would have been inexplicable in ancient cultures – even today people believe that cats know and see a lot more than they choose to reveal.

PRAYERS AND PROMISES

In Japan, the Maneki-neko has its own shrine. Its legend began when some Samurai followed a beckoning cat to a shrine, where they took shelter from a storm. They spread the fame of the temple, and people brought their cats to be buried there and prayed for the feline souls and luck in their own lives. The Romans kept cats as pets, and a Roman bride would make a sacrifice and gift to appease the house cats in her new home. Ancient Egyptians wore amulets in the shape of a cat or a cat's head. These were buried with them for continued protection.

Left: Bast, the original Egyptian lucky cat
Right: Black cat, for good luck or bad
Below: Dick Whittington's fairytale cat

TRUE COLORS

In Britain, a black cat is a lucky omen, welcome at weddings and invited to cross everyone's path. Dick Whittington's cat, who set him on the road to prosperity, is usually depicted as black. Black cats in medieval Britain, however, were seen as familiars, imps in disguise, and made to suffer cruel torture and death. In some areas of Europe and in North America this history has not been forgotten, and the white cat is seen as lucky. In Russia the Russian Blue is a lucky symbol, and in Thailand another gray cat, the ancient Korat, is often given to brides to bring good fortune.

GARRICK THEATRE
LONDON.
Telephone No. Temple Bar 8713.
Commencing Boxing-Day, Dec. 26th.

DICK WHITTINGTON
PANTOMIME
TWICE DAILY AT 2-0 and 7-45

CATS AT WAR

Through the ages, cats have fought both for armies and for causes, as well as being innocent victims. Here are some of the names in the lists.

Cats starred in the battle of Pelusium in 525 B.C. Legend has it that the invading Persian army strapped cats to their shields. Faced with the feline phalanx, the Egyptians downed spears and fled rather than hurt a sacred animal, and Pelusium was taken without a blow.

This century, cats were the victims of Kenyan strife. In the 1950s, Mau Mau guerillas killed colonials' cats to warn the owners of their coming demise.

GUARD DUTY

Usually, cats play less central roles. Frederick the Great of Prussia, although preferring canine pets, appreciated cats, and gave orders that hundreds be posted to keep the army stores vermin-free. In World War II, the British Ministry of Supply asked the public to volunteer their pets for the same task, and patriotic owners across the country sent in cats by the basketful in response.

Left: Wildcat stirring things up as usual
Above right: Simon and his comrades
Right: Prussian ruler Frederick the Great

ACTIVE SERVICE

Cats are not always confined to base. Simon, H.M.S. *Amethyst*'s ratter, carried on undeterred as the ship was attacked by the Chinese and dashed down the Yangtze to freedom. He was awarded the Dickin medal, the animals' Victoria Cross.

Another cat who never gives up is Wildcat, freedom fighter from *Freedom*, a British anarchist publication. She has a typically feline approach to the fight for justice: her own strongly held moral code and an almost total disregard for what others think of her.

SHIP'S CATS

Cats find a place on ships as good luck mascots, rodent controlers, or the pets of captain and crew.

Ship's cats have a long history. Rodents are a plague on ships, because there are so many nooks where they can hide. Cats spread from Egypt as pets on ships, and crossed the Atlantic the same way. In New England, there are high numbers of polydactylic cats (with extra toes), which are descendants of some ship's cats with this characteristic.

CRUISE LIFE

Much as a ship's cat might like to spend the days sunning itself on deck, most must earn their keep with a sizeable catch before being allowed to relax.

Some ship's cats do live very adventurous lives, however. When Scott departed for the Antarctic, the ship's black cat sailed too, but wisely it did not go on overland. Cats are also often spoiled by crews, and even treated as humans. The sailors of the *Hecate* entered Able Seacat Fred Wunpound's name on a census form, and were very offended when his right to vote was refused. They believed that Fred brought them luck: on one trip that he missed, computers crashed, machines broke down, and an engine blew up.

Opposite: Tao-Tai on board the Sagamore
Left: The Discovery cat heading for the Antarctic in its own personal hammock
Below: Paddy-pawed polydactylic cat

PART OF THE FURNITURE

Some cats will not even leave a sinking ship. When the *Liberty* ran aground off Cornwall, the ship's cat refused to leave. He sat tight for six weeks until he was netted by salvage workers. They duly named the steadfast – some might say stubborn – cat Carlsen, after the captain who had refused to leave his ship, the doomed *Flying Enterprise*.

When the shipping group Furness Withy decided to sell one of their ships, the *Sagamore*, the ship's cat was listed among the fixtures and fittings. The Italian purchasers were not sure about taking on Princess Truban Tao-Tai, but the Siamese had been on the

ship for 16 years, and could not be expected to adapt to a new home. Eventually, it was made a clause of the sale contract that the new owners must take the cat and guarantee to keep her happy.

I N D E X

ACKNOWLEDGMENTS

Key: t=top, b=bottom, l=left, r=right, c=center

DK Pictures
Jane Burton: 26bl, 40-41, 47t, 59b
Marc Henrie: 9, 21, 22, 24-25, 28, 29t, b, 30, 31tl, b, 32-33
Dave King: 5, 8, 31tr, 44-45
Steve Gorton and Tim Ridley: 7, 26cr, 46
Matthew Ward: 27b

13t is reproduced Courtesy of the Trustees of the British Museum

Agency Pictures
Bridgeman Art Library: front jacket bl, 10, 11t, 12, 13b   E.T. Archive: 17tl, 51b
Mary Evans: 14, 15, 16, 38-39, 47b, 51t   Kobal Collection: 18, 19bl
Ronald Grant Archive: 19tr   Royal Library, Windsor Castle: 11b
Michael Holford: front jacket br, 23t, 50   Popperfoto: 17tr   Scala: 23b
SIPA Press: 42   Syndication International: 35, 43

Cataerobic center on page 34 supplied by Canac Pet Products

Picture Research: Diana Morris
Design Assistance: Patrizio Semproni
Illustration: Stephen Lings, Clive Spong

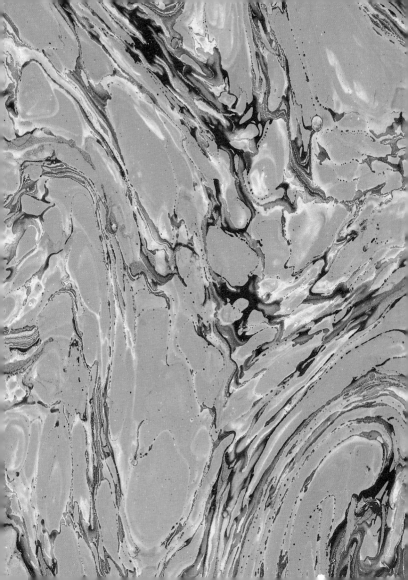